VALLE CRUCIS

The Shull's family cemetery (1979)

VALLE CRUCIS

Text by David W. Yates
and
Photographs by William A. Bake

JOHN F. BLAIR, PUBLISHER
WINSTON-SALEM, NORTH CAROLINA

Library of Congress
Cataloging-in-Publication Data

Yates, David W. (David Wayne), 1962–
         Valle Crucis / David W. Yates and
         William A. Bake.
              p.   cm.
         ISBN 0-89587-203-X (alk. paper)
         1. Valle Crucis Region (N.C.)—Pictorial works.
     2. Valle Crucis Region (N.C.)—History.   3. Historic
     buildings—North Carolina—Valle Crucis Region—
     Pictorial works.   I. Bake, William A., 1938– .   II. Title.
     F264.V35V38   1997
     975.6'843—dc21   97–19071

Rominger Road

DEDICATION

Jerry E. Yates

1967–89

To my beloved brother, who loved Valle Crucis as much as I do

FROSTY MORNING

The Watauga River

Along the River Road (1978)

AUTUMN TRAIL

Near Hanging Rock

CONTENTS

Acknowledgments
i x

Photographer's Note
x i

Touring Valle Crucis
x i i i

A Crooked Road to the Past
3

Clark's Creek area

Along Broadstone Road (1978)

Acknowledgments

I take great pleasure in thanking my friends and neighbors in Valle Crucis for the time, support, and assistance they gave me, for their family stories, and for opening their old family scrapbooks for me. I thank Bill Bake for his beautiful photographs and his creative ideas and direction. I am honored to have worked with such a talented artist. I thank my parents for answering my endless questions about the good old days and for helping me understand the Valle Crucis my ancestors knew.

Finally, I thank my wonderful wife, Roberta, for her patience, for her boundless optimism and encouragement, and for believing in me.

Without all of these people, this book, this dream of mine, would never have come true.

Overlooking Broadstone Road

Photographer's Note

Although most of the photographs included here were made specifically for this book in late 1996 and early 1997, some date back almost twenty years to the time I became a resident of Watauga County.

I used two sizes of film: 35mm and 4 x 5 inch. For the 35mm images, I used Kodachrome 64 film until 1993. After that, Kodak Lumière and Fuji Velvia became my films of choice. In the 4 x 5-inch size, I employed the full variety of Ektachrome films, including tungsten film corrected to daylight.

The cameras I used are old models. In 35mm, I used Pentax LX and ME Super cameras, both dating from 1981, along with 20mm, 40–80mm, 150mm, and 300mm Pentax lenses. For the 4 x 5-inch work, I used my trusty companion, a 1979 British MPP Mark V technical camera with wide-angle, regular, and long-focus lenses. Generally, I prefer to use only color-correction filters and a polarizer. A tripod is always necessary for landscape photography.

I might add that more than equipment and technical ability is needed when creating visual essays about places. Knowledge of cultural and natural history is essential. For example, one must understand that Valle Crucis is an expression of the Jeffersonian ideal. It is also important to know the natural aspects of the Southern Highlands. Knowledge such as this connects the images and those who see them.

Finally, there must be feeling, a sense of visual poetry. As Antoine de Saint-Exupéry put it, "The physical drama itself cannot touch us until some one points out its spiritual sense."

My special thanks goes to David Yates, without whose vision and persistence this book would not have been published.

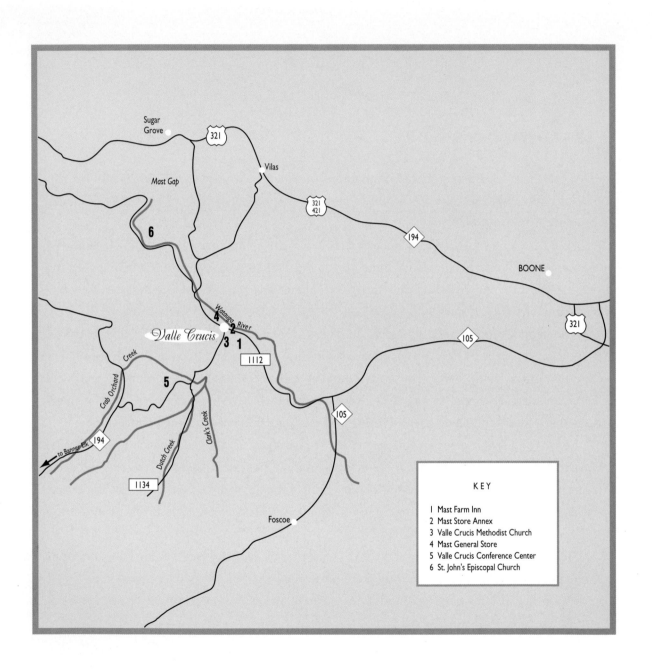

Sugar Grove

321

Vilas

Mast Gap

321
421

194

BOONE

6

321

Watauga River

4

Valle Crucis

2
3 1

105

1112

Creek

Crab Orchard

5

105

to Banner Elk 194

Clark's Creek

Dutch Creek

1134

Foscoe

KEY

1 Mast Farm Inn
2 Mast Store Annex
3 Valle Crucis Methodist Church
4 Mast General Store
5 Valle Crucis Conference Center
6 St. John's Episcopal Church

Near the Mast Farm Inn

Touring Valle Crucis

You can find Valle Crucis on a road map of North Carolina. But to truly understand the place, you should know that it lies in a level valley along the Watauga River, which flows northwest from its source on nearby Grandfather Mountain (elevation 5,964 feet). Just to the west, Dutch Creek, Clark's Creek, and Crab Orchard Creek have their own level valley, which drains into the Watauga. These fertile valleys determined the location of Valle Crucis and the Valle Crucis Episcopal Mission.

Driving into Valle Crucis, you will follow water. If, like many people, you are approaching from N.C. 105 and heading down the "lower" river valley, turn onto Broadstone Road at the light and the Valle Crucis sign. Immediately on your right is the Watauga River, which the road closely parallels for two miles before diverging to avoid low-lying farmland. You will pass a sign for Bluestone Lodge, a new, lovely bed-and-breakfast that sits high on a mountain. You will pass Camp Broadstone on the left, then two large white farmhouses on the right. You will then pass River Run Farm, a new thoroughbred farm. A half-mile farther, you will arrive at the Mast Farm Inn before reaching the Mast Store Annex, then the Mast General Store.

A few visitors arrive from Banner Elk on winding N.C. 194 North. From that direction, the road follows switchbacks for eight hundred feet down a steep escarpment and travels past the Valle Crucis Conference Center and the Inn at the Taylor House into the "upper" valley formed by Dutch Creek, Clark's Creek, and Crab Orchard Creek. The road then joins the "lower" valley and Broadstone Road near the Mast General Store. The views and rural structures along this road make it the most historic and scenic route into Valle Crucis. The old road from Banner Elk was once the closest route to a railroad and outside supplies at Elk Park, a hard sixteen-mile climb from Valle Crucis on a muddy road.

If you continue to follow the river and N.C. 194 North through the "lower" valley past the Mast General Store, you will pass the historic Frank Baird (pronounced Beard) Farm, then cross the Watauga River. In two-thirds of a mile, look for another historic structure, St. John's Episcopal Church, a white clapboard country church visible in the distance across the river valley to your left. You can reach it by turning left onto Mast Gap Road, then left again onto Herb Thomas Road. If you continue on Mast Gap Road, you reach U.S. 321.

Although they are technically not part of the "valle," the homesteads along the River Road are considered part of the Valle Crucis area. The River Road is one-half mile past the Mast General Store, on the left just before crossing the bridge over the Watauga River. Following this route will give you the closest continual views of the river. Along this road are beautiful old homesteads which were far enough from the central part of the valley to form their own community and build their own store. This route takes you past another bed-and-breakfast inn, the Inn at Valle Crucis. Just before the road joins U.S. 321, the area's only remaining mill sits on the Watauga River. It is part of the Ward family homestead, one of the oldest in the area.

Continuing straight on N.C. 194 will take you to U.S. 321/421. To the left, U.S. 321 plunges along with the Watauga River into Tennessee. To the right, U.S. 421 heads into Boone.

VALLE CRUCIS

THE VALLEY AWAITS THE SUN

October morning, Baird's Creek area

Overlooking Baird's Creek

A Crooked Road to the Past

*H*igh in the Blue Ridge Mountains of North Carolina, between the shrouded peaks of Grandfather Mountain and the town of Boone, you must cross the Watauga River. Here, you will come upon two road signs. One reminds you that you are on an official "Scenic Byway." The other simply invites you to turn onto a narrow road—the road to Valle Crucis.

If you accept this quiet invitation, as thousands do each year, you will drive along the river with mountains rising steeply on each side. Over the guardrails, you will begin to catch glimpses of a hidden alpine valley. If it's early, you will probably see an ocean of fog with hills rising like

RAINY DAY ON THE RIVER ROAD

The Watauga River

The Watauga River

islands out of the mist. You will soon arrive in a small, historic pioneer village that appears much like it did a century ago.

You have found Valle Crucis, one of the South's greatest treasures.

The valley has changed remarkably little in the last century and a half. It consists of a broad "lower" valley formed by several miles of the Watauga River and a small "upper" valley formed by three creeks. These three small creeks and the surrounding valley are responsible for the spot's beautiful name.

In the early 1840s, Levi Ives, the second Episcopal bishop of North Carolina, looked down into this same isolated valley. From the wooded hillside, Bishop Ives saw three creeks that

4

Overlooking the Watauga River

appeared to form a St. Andrew's cross. He named the place Valle Crucis—Latin for Vale of the Cross.

In 1889, Susan Fenimore Cooper, daughter of James Fenimore Cooper, described this early expedition into "the Valle" in *Missionary Life in Valle Crucis*:

> The valley, entirely shut in by forest-clad mountains, was watered by three limpid streams, two of them leaping down the hillsides in foaming cascades. The principal stream, formed by the junction, after a short course of about two miles, after passing through a narrow gorge, threw itself into the Watauga. The waters rushing over the rocky bed of the stream, and the many lesser brooks leaping down the mountainside, filled the air with an unceasing murmur, now loud and full, then more gentle and subdued. It was this secluded valley which, from the cross-like form of the three streams at their junction, was now to receive the name of Valle Crucis.

Steep, wooded mountains protect the calm, fertile meadows from the rest of the world. It's not a large place, but it is remarkable in its beauty and its historical importance—its beauty in its very isolation. Springtime brings a burst of wildflowers, rhododendrons, and mountain laurel. Summers are cool and breezy. Fall colors rival any in New England. And, although deep in the South, winters here shimmer with heavy, silent snow.

The secret of the valley's seductive appeal remains elusive. The beauty here varies from the dramatic to the quaint, from brilliant colors to black-and-white moonlit nights following a heavy snow. The valley is both majestic and quietly graceful. To live in Valle Crucis or to rest here a few days is to experience a soothing array of colors, smells, and sounds, all seemingly designed to induce calm in the human soul. From scenic mountaintop views to vignettes of life in this mountain farming village, from the smell of apple butter being made in a cast-iron pot to the reassuring sound of 150-year-old wooden church floors creaking under your feet, it is an unforgettable place.

Clark's Creek area

Civilization seems far away. The valley has never been a bustling center of commercial activity and is home to only a few homesteads, farms, and businesses. Because of its hidden nature, Valle Crucis has become a national historical treasure. It was the first rural area in North Carolina granted legal protection as a Historic District. It is home to several sites that have been placed on the National Register of Historic Places. The Mast Farm homestead was the first site in Watauga County to be so recognized. This old homestead, now a bed-and-breakfast, consists of thirteen remarkably well-preserved buildings constructed as early as 1812. The Mast General Store, built in 1883, is one of the oldest and best-preserved general stores in the country. The Valle Crucis Episcopal Mission, begun under the direction of Bishop Ives in the 1840s, was the site of the first Anglican monastery created since the sixteenth century. Each of these sites is a living museum that offers a unique opportunity for a glimpse of life as it existed a century ago.

————

Being just a little far away and hard to get to has protected the valley over the years. Thanks to its narrow, winding roads, long winters, and cool summers, it has remained a place that most people only visit. Since the early 1900s, Valle Crucis has been known for its hospitality. Several of its old homesteads began to board vacationers almost a century ago and are now romantic bed-and-breakfast inns. No more than a few hundred people have ever lived here at any given time, but since the nineteenth century, something has drawn visitors in droves. Much of Valle Crucis appears as if it were lifted untouched out of the previous century and placed here as a reminder of times past. It has been called "magnificent," "dreamy," "glorious," and "a little community blessed with good people and a knack for making folks feel welcome."

I call it home. Inevitably, almost every visitor starts to wonder what it would be like to live in such a place. I never hesitate to tell them. My family came to Valle Crucis over 150 years ago. Five generations are buried here. My grandmother, Allie Yates, who died in 1994, was born in Valle Crucis in 1899—well before cars, telephones, or electricity arrived. She filled my childhood with stories of pioneer life that most of us can experience only through books or photographs.

The Hodges farm, Baird's Creek area (1985)

Rubin Walker Road

Along Herb Thomas Road

My love for and memories of Valle Crucis were shaped not only by childhood days spent with my brother fishing, lurking about old, abandoned houses, and loafing around the Mast General Store, but also by my grandparents' stories of wagon rides to pick blueberries on Grandfather Mountain, of the struggles of Dr. Perry, the only local doctor, and of the characters who stayed at the Mast Farm Inn, where my grandmother worked as a girl. She knew the bishops and missionaries who struggled to rebuild the Valle Crucis Episcopal Mission at the turn of the century. She attended their schools and raised her family here.

Likewise, thanks to my family, my imagination is fired by images of a Valle Crucis few visitors know: a Valle Crucis isolated from the advances that made life easier, a Valle Crucis where children died from lack of access to simple medical treatment, a Valle Crucis destroyed by a flood which tore through the valley decades before I was born. This flood swept away everything in sight—people, farm animals, houses, churches. My grandmother described to me in vivid detail how she watched the river rise over one bridge in the "lower" valley near the Mast Farm Inn, and how the bridge, built to remain solid even when underwater, held fast. It

Farming the "upper" valley in the early 1900s
VALLE CRUCIS CONFERENCE CENTER

held, that is, until the haystacks came along. The river, obviously angry that the bridge was winning, began to spread into the fields and pick up haystacks. Entire fields of haystacks piled against the bridge. The river, haystacks bobbing like apples, created its own dam. With haystacks piled thirty feet high, it exploded the bridge and sent the whole wall of haystacks and mangled bridge in search of another challenge. I still get scared when the river rises.

When the idea for attempting to preserve Valle Crucis through this book came to me, I immediately asked Dr. William A. Bake for help. Bill has the unparalleled ability to take an object or scene we have seen every day and capture beauty our own eyes simply do not perceive. If you have ever seen one of Bill's photographs of a scene you recognize, you know what I mean. I have stood with my jaw dropped before Bill's photographs, only to find that I have breezed by those same scenes for twenty-five years. Whether a barn, a mountain, or a tobacco field, Bill's

A FINE DAY

Coopers' barn

subjects draw you into a secret world. Bill has photographed Valle Crucis for over twenty years. Not only has he preserved scenes we may never see again, but without saying a word, he convinces us that we have never appreciated just how beautiful those scenes really were.

As you drive down the valley, you will notice small cabins dotting the hillsides. As the narrow river valley broadens into fertile meadows, you will see large, old homesteads and farms. You will pass a popular summer camp, Camp Broadstone, where I worked as a teenager. On the banks of the river, you will see River Run Farm, a thoroughbred farm that rivals the most beautiful of its kind in Kentucky.

HARVESTED AND READY

Cove Creek Valley

River Run Farm

Soon thereafter, you will arrive at one of the oldest and best-preserved pioneer homesteads in the South, now a cozy bed-and-breakfast inn nestled against the side of the mountain. After staying at this old inn, a writer for the *New York Times* said, "The Mast Farm Inn is about as close as you can get to defining the word *homespun*."

Although the rambling green-and-white Victorian bed-and-breakfast now bustles with guests, I remember the old homestead as it was during my childhood in the 1970s, an elaborate playground, abandoned and full of dark rooms with numbers on the doors, old trunks, and mysterious farm utensils. I spent days exploring the old buildings, swinging from the rope hanging in

FORESIGHT REWARDED

The Mast Farm Inn

The Mast Farm Inn

the top of the old barn, and searching the surrounding fields for arrowheads. My imagination was fueled by my grandmother's stories of the characters who stayed in the inn when she worked here as a teenager during the early 1900s, and of Joe Mast, the last of the family to live on the farm. Many of the rooms are now named after people at the inn almost a century ago, including my grandmother, "Miss Allie."

THE MAST FARM INN

In the late 1700s, Joseph Mast walked all the way from Pennsylvania and settled on much of the land that is now Valle Crucis. Around 1810, his son David built the two-room log cabin which now sits facing the main house at the Mast Farm. Three generations of the family resided in this cabin. Like most Valle Crucis residents, the Masts raised corn, grain, sheep, cattle, and food for the family.

The Masts built more farm buildings over the years, including the large barn across the road from the main house. Of necessity, the farm was designed to be self-sufficient and self-contained. By the early 1900s, at least sixteen different buildings were part of the old mountain farmstead. Remarkably, thirteen remain today. Most of the buildings in the meadow were used for livestock, for the storage of hay and grain, and for tobacco curing. The springhouse, smokehouse, icehouse, blacksmith shop, woodworking shop, and wash house were on the south side of the road adjacent to the cabin, tucked away from the wind. On the north side of the road, almost directly across from the small garage, a large harness shed once stood. A pen for hogs sat where the small pond behind the blacksmith shop is now located.

David's son Andrew began building the main house around 1880. Andrew's son, D. Finley Mast, completed it in 1896. A photo of the house in the early 1900s shows a sign stating simply, "BROOKSIDE FARM, D. FINLEY MAST, ONE HALF MILE TO POST OFFICE." Originally, the main house consisted of only the part closest to the road—three stories high, with two rooms on each floor. Like most large homes with open flames for cooking, it had a detached kitchen.

The blacksmith shop, which also required an open fire, was located in a separate log structure. The building for curing meat was separate as well. Laundry was done in large cast-iron pots of boiling water in the wash house by the creek, safely away from the house.

In the early 1900s, Finley and his wife, Josephine, began to make additions to the house and to operate it as an inn. Over a period of about twenty-five years, five different symmetrical additions were completed, ultimately comprising thirteen bedrooms—and one bathroom.

The earliest known photograph of the main house at the Mast Farm, believed to have been taken around 1900. The upstairs porch facing the road is now enclosed.

COURTESY OF FRANCIS AND SIBYL PRESSLEY

In the early 1900s, when my grandmother was a child and railroads and improved roads brought visitors to nearby towns such as Blowing Rock, the farm, indeed the whole valley, became a haven for flatlanders escaping the heat and the hustle of city life. Guests came from as far north as Washington, D.C., and as far south as New Orleans and Florida to stay with Finley and Josephine Mast. After huge family-style dinners, the men generally sat on the porch

The Mast Farm Inn

The Mast Farm Inn

smoking their pipes, while the women gathered inside. Well before automobiles sped around the curves of the road, playing children had to share the lawn with grazing horses. There was a well-worn path across the meadow, where visitors walked to a wooden swinging footbridge crossing the Watauga River.

The Mast garden

In her autobiography, *Quiet Pilgrimage*, Elizabeth Gray Vining wrote of traveling from Chapel Hill, North Carolina, to the Mast Farm during summer in the early 1900s:

Though we went to Valle Crucis by car and found modern plumbing and electric lights in the old house, going there was like stepping back into another era—a time when the Jeffersonian ideal of American life prevailed. Almost everything that we ate was grown on the place. Every day there appeared on the long, white-clothed table at which we all sat: fried chicken, ham, homemade sausage, hot biscuits and spoon bread, home-churned butter, thick cream, cottage cheese, vegetables just out of the garden, ever-bearing strawberries, applesauce, peaches. Once I counted twenty different dishes. . . .

The conversation around that table was good. There were keen minds, aware of questions of the day, people who had traveled, people interested in folklore and the changing customs of the mountain life.

The Masts were known far and wide for their hospitality and their food. My grandmother remembered how visitors arrived in buggies and later in cars on Sunday afternoons. The reason was buttermilk, which Josephine Mast served outside on long tables by the springhouse.

In those days, the loom house on the property housed up to a half-dozen looms. My grandmother, Josephine Mast, and other local women were master craftswomen by today's standards. They learned

Carloads of people came to the inn for Sunday lunch and Josephine Mast's buttermilk. The tables are in front of the springhouse. The smokehouse is visible on the hillside above.
COURTESY OF FRANCIS AND SIBYL PRESSLEY

to make clothing, quilts, and anything else that could be used on the farm. My grandmother could knit, crochet, and make rare lace and quilt patterns passed down from her European ancestors. Josephine Mast was a master weaver famous for her skill and generosity. As Elizabeth Gray Vining wrote,

> Aunt Josie was a remarkable woman in any time or place. A slender, vigorous, gray-haired little figure filled with energy and warmth, she ran her part of the farm—the vegetable garden, the dairy and the house, with its dozen or so paying guests—with almost careless competence. She mothered the people of the countryside, who were forever coming to her with their troubles, which ranged from ailments (which she treated with herb remedies) and hunger (which she fed with baskets of food) to questions about the directions of their lives or the resolution of family conflicts. In her spare time she relaxed by going into the loom house and weaving several inches of bedspread, rug, or bag.

Josephine Mast at work in the loom house
COURTESY OF FRANCIS AND SIBYL PRESSLEY

When President Woodrow Wilson's daughter, Jessie, was to be married, Josephine gathered neighbors to help weave spreads and rugs for Jessie's room in the White House. According to newspaper reports of the time, the president's family was so impressed by the work that it redecorated the room around the weavings. Some of Josephine's weavings are now in the Smithsonian.

Finley and Josephine Mast had two sons. Joe, the son who stayed on the farm, was blind by the time he was a young adult. According to my grandmother, Joe attached strings between the buildings in order to find his way around the farm. Later, with typical mountain ingenuity, he abandoned the strings and created his own personal method of getting from place to place on the farm. My father remembers Joe, on hands and knees, pulling grass from hand-made trails between the farm buildings. He used these trails, always plucked free of grass, as guides. Joe overcame his handicap and was able to chop wood and perform other tasks seemingly impossible without the benefit of sight.

He and his wife, Edna, continued to run the house as a successful inn until the 1950s. The main house often was so full that Joe slept upstairs in the loom house to make room for guests. Generations of visitors returned to the gracious house.

The old Mast barn (1979)

After Edna died and Joe became ill, Edna's maid Nell, my family, and other neighbors helped take care of Joe. My father often stayed with Joe as he grew old and unable to fend for himself. As his health continued to decline, he moved out of the old house in 1964. He died in 1969. Joe and Edna had no children, and no one in the family stepped forward to carry on the tradition of hospitality.

Elizabeth Gray Vining visited Valle Crucis again in 1968 and wrote,

> The house was closed and wore a dejected, unlived-in look. Bedraggled white curtains in the windows suggested that someone had gone out and shut the door on it, just as it was, when the old people died. The spring house and woodshed were empty, the washhouse crumbling, the loom house filled with old wheelbarrows and rusty tools; a half-finished bedspread on the loom was gray with age and dust and festooned with cobwebs. At some time a flood must have changed the course of the brook and the forget-me-nots were gone.
>
> Up on the hill, well-fenced, well cared for, in contrast, was the family burial ground.

In 1972, the United States Department of the Interior evaluated the property at the request of the Mast family. The department's representative wrote,

> The numerous buildings that make up the Mast Farm, each expressive of its function, represent vividly the wide variety of operations necessary to a self-sustaining farm complex. The weaving house is particularly interesting, both because . . . "it is an example of log construction which reached its finest development in North Carolina," and because it was the original dwelling around which the farm grew up. With this building as a nucleus, the farm illustrates the progression of an enterprising pioneer family from this rude early house on a small homestead to a larger, more comfortable house, the seat of much larger land holdings. This complex includes one of the most complete and best preserved groups of nineteenth-century farm buildings in western North Carolina.

Cool Springs, Beech Mountain

The farm was placed on the National Register of Historic Places. At that time, the loom house still contained several working looms, but the main house and many of the outbuildings were in serious disrepair. The family put the farm up for sale.

The Paul Lackey family bought the property from Joe's heirs in 1980. After beginning some renovations, the Lackeys sold it to Francis and Sibyl Pressley in 1984. Francis and Sibyl rescued the old homestead. They first renovated and moved into the loom house, then began the painstaking process of renovating the main house according to the strict historic guidelines for National Register properties. They opened the main house to guests in 1985 and later renovated the granary, the blacksmith shop, and the woodworking shop.

A year's worth of meticulous work resulted in the facility you see today and earned them the Gertrude S. Carraway Award of Merit from the Historic Preservation Foundation of North Carolina. Likewise, their hospitality landed the inn in the prestigious *Innkeepers' Register*, a publication containing inns known for their hospitality, service, and historical or other special interest.

The Pressleys served family-style meals and grew much of their produce on the farm. Much like the Masts in years gone by, they borrowed recipes from neighbors and friends.

Francis and Sibyl Pressley retired as innkeepers in 1996 and sold the inn to the Schoenfeldt family, which plans to carry the Masts' tradition of hospitality into another century. If you get a chance to stay in this grand old inn, you will find that it is operated much the same way the Masts ran it almost a century ago. The rooms are furnished with period antiques. Guests eat freshly prepared meals around big tables, exchange stories with their fellow travelers, sit on the porch, and take walks around the farm. Fortunately, they no longer have to share a single bathroom with a houseful of guests. Progress does have its advantages, even in Valle Crucis.

As "the Valle" eased into the twentieth century, residents needed groceries, building supplies, and other goods they could not grow or make. Most local people made their living farming or cutting timber from the forested hillsides. The community was big enough to support several sawmills and gristmills, two general stores, a garage, and, believe it or not, a bank.

The Mast Store Annex, located beyond the Mast Farm Inn, was once the competitor of the famous establishment a bit farther down the road, the Mast General Store. C. D. "Squire" Taylor, the local farmer and entrepreneur who built the present-day Inn at the Taylor House, named this new store the Valle Crucis Company. He eventually sold it to another local family, the Farthings. This store also served as Valle Crucis's post office for over thirty years. In a fitting

The Mast Farm Inn

twist of fate for such a small village, Aubyn Farthing's daughter, Mary Hazel, married H. W. Mast, the son of competing Mast General Store owner W. W. Mast.

The Mast Store Annex sits across the road from Valle Crucis Methodist Church and the former Valle Crucis Bank. Beside the church, built in 1894, is the small house that was once the bank. Several prominent citizens pooled their money and chartered the bank in 1913. Many local folks, including my great-grandparents and grandparents, used this bank until it closed just prior to the Great Depression.

RURAL LIVES

Valle Crucis Methodist Church and old barn (1985)

Along Broadstone Road (1978)

The Valle Crucis Methodist Church and Mast Store Annex

Toward Valle Landing, the Valle Crucis School, and the Mast Store Annex

For over a century, in addition to being the source of everything "from cradles to caskets," the Mast General Store, located beyond the Mast Store Annex, has been the unofficial cultural center of Valle Crucis. Just step inside the worn front door and it's easy to understand why the ten-thousand-square-foot store was placed on the National Register of Historic Places and has become one of the most famous general stores in the United States. It is filled with the stuff of childhood dreams.

EARLY RISER

The Mast General Store

The Mast General Store (1978)

During my grandparents' youth, the store housed the local doctor. It still contains the post office, on the left as you walk in. Here, a real person hand-stamps all mail and sorts it into small mailboxes. I have often felt the envious looks of visitors watching me struggle with the ancient combination lock as I attempt to get my mail. As local families have done for a century, you can walk in on a cool fall morning, back up against the eight-foot-tall potbellied stove, and warm your vital parts.

ALLEN MAST

The Mast General Store

The Mast General Store

Here, stories are told. As a boy, I met my friends at the stove. We drank Cokes and talked about fishing and told jokes. We played checkers. Our parents—and their parents—had done the same. We tried to get into trouble, but, in a small store in a small valley, it never seemed to work. We were safe. We seldom bought anything except Cokes—and fishhooks.

The coffee is still a nickel. You can still sit down in a rocking chair and play a game of

The Mast General Store

checkers—with bottle caps for checkers. If you actually need to buy anything, you will probably find it.

Squire Taylor constructed the store in 1883 and sold it to William Wellington "W. W." Mast at the turn of the century. The Masts operated the store for the next seventy years. The proprietors included W. W.'s son Howard Wellington Mast and Howard's son H. W. Mast, Jr., known locally as "H" (spelled A-I-T-C-H, if you ask). The Masts stocked the store with everything local farmers needed, from food and clothes to hardware, feed, and farm supplies. They sold saddles, harnesses, and horseshoes. They sold fabric, ribbon, and other supplies needed in any home. They sold on credit. They bartered and bought and sold local farm produce. You can still see the small trapdoor leading to the coop beneath the floor where chickens were kept. Upstairs, you can see hooks in the ceiling where country hams once hung.

The Masts also told very bad jokes.

H. W. Mast, Jr., finally sold the store in 1972, after farming in Valle Crucis had declined but before large numbers of visitors began arriving. The store had several owners, none successful, before John Cooper purchased it in 1980. John and his family had been regular visitors to Valle Crucis from Florida during the 1970s. The store had been open intermittently for several years and was closed by the end of the decade. In what most would consider a romantic but risky undertaking, John and his wife, Faye, sold their car to raise money and purchased the old store and its inventory. They and their two young children moved from Florida, built an apartment upstairs in the old store, and started a new life as purveyors of their very own general store.

As they set out to renovate the old store, John and Faye sought to maintain what they had loved: its charm. They changed only as much as was necessary to save the store. They sold cattle feed, locally grown produce, honey, flour, meal, jellies, jams, and locally made crafts. They sold shoes, clothes, groceries, and hardware.

Just as important, they rekindled the spirit of Valle Crucis's old friend. Locals gathered around as if the store had never lost a step. Children again rode their bikes to the store for Cokes and fishhooks. Even better for me, the store became a home to teenagers, who worked here during the summers and on weekends. Along with many others, including the Coopers' children, the Masts' children, and Bill Bake's daughter, I shoveled coal, sorted mail, stocked shelves, delivered feed to local farmers, and smiled at the envious visitors. My memories of summers in the old store are among my favorites.

The Coopers saved much of the old inventory, which still lines the top shelves. You can see old advertising posters that have covered the same space on the walls for decades. You can see the old cash registers and the old safe, which was once carried away by thieves.

IT MADE A GOOD SLED

In an old barn

If you are lucky, you can catch former owner "H" Mast or his son and my oldest friend, Allen Mast, helping out behind the cash register. If you hang around long enough, one of them, like their forefathers before them, will tell you a very bad joke.

And except for the old pine casket upstairs, which is no longer for sale, you can still buy just about anything you might ever need.

Behind the store is the old Valle Crucis Schoolhouse, where my grandmother attended classes for a time and where my father attended high school. In 1907, when this school was built, it was the largest in the area. The local paper noted, "The splendid new school building, erected by the good people of Valle Crucis, has been completed and neatly painted. It is one of

THE LITTLE RED SCHOOLHOUSE

January afternoon

the best in the county." It served as the primary school in the area for over thirty years and housed Valle Crucis's first high school. By the time the Coopers reopened the Mast General Store in 1980, the old schoolhouse, abandoned for decades, had fallen into disrepair and was being used as a tobacco barn. It was rescued and now houses a local artist.

Two miles down the river from the Mast General Store, past the historic Frank Baird Farm, perched high on a hill overlooking the Watauga River, sits St. John's Episcopal Church, a small church of simple, stunning beauty. Built by early Episcopal missionaries, the little church has survived the ravages of nature for over a century and a half.

ANOTHER SNOW COMING

The Frank Baird Farm

Frank Baird (1988)

The Frank Baird barn (1977)

In the Frank Baird barn

VALLE CRUCIS

The Frank Baird farm

ST. JOHN'S EPISCOPAL CHURCH

Before the original Valle Crucis Episcopal Mission closed in the 1860s, one of the last acts of the Reverend William West Skiles, a principal figure at the mission since the late 1840s, was to supervise the building of St. John's Episcopal Church. With the donation of materials, labor, and money—a third of which Skiles gave himself—the missionary fulfilled his dream in 1860. Skiles began holding monthly services in the white Gothic wooden church, which the bishop came to consecrate in 1862. That same year, Skiles died. His body was buried beneath a tree beside his beloved church.

Moved higher on the hillside in 1882, the church remains a monument to Skiles's devotion. As the reigning bishop once said in an address to the Convention of North Carolina, "The Church, Gothic, and with windows of stained glass, would anywhere be a pleasing object, but in that sequestered, and picturesque spot, with the bright waters of the Watauga washing the foot of the hill on which it is built, and the high mountains standing as a guard around it, it is a touching, and appropriate memorial of that man of God, the Rev. Mr. Skiles, to whom its erection was so long a darling object, and by whose unrelaxed efforts, this was at length accomplished."

St. John's Episcopal Church

As late as the 1970s, in the cool shadows of the church grounds, my family often joined other Valle Crucis residents in filling long tables with homemade food for Sunday-afternoon picnics. Then, in the early 1980s, the unthinkable happened. Vandals stole all but three of the beloved church's old wooden pews and ripped the decorative woodwork off the altar. My family helped in the local effort to rebuild the pews and re-create the delicate woodcarvings of the altar.

The church is now used for special services, concerts, and weddings—including my own, during which we were compelled to decorate the simple church only by opening the windows and filling the inside with wildflowers. A neighbor played traditional music on a hammered dulcimer.

With its worn wooden floors, walked on for 150 years, St. John's invites visitors to be reverent. Musicians cherish the church for its haunting acoustics. Others prize it for its simple Gothic design and its special place in local history.

If you want to see the picturesque "upper" valley that gave the Vale of the Cross its name, follow the winding road that intersects the main road between the Mast General Store and the Mast Store Annex. You will soon reach the Inn at the Taylor House, one of the country's most beautiful inns.

On at least one occasion, a stay at the Inn at the Taylor House literally changed someone's life. A few years ago, a young professional from the city came for a weekend. He began to relax, to take walks, to reexamine his place in the world. In the inn's magnificent setting, overlooking the fields of the original Valle Crucis Episcopal Mission, he decided to extend his stay past the weekend into the following week, then into another week. Ultimately, this young man decided to abandon his urban struggle. He later entered the seminary and now serves in an Episcopal parish in the southwestern United States. Never let it be said that humans are not affected by their physical surroundings.

C. D. "Squire" Taylor built the grand, old fourteen-room house overlooking his farm in 1911. While the Gilded Age passed Valle Crucis unnoticed, Squire did his share to bring

THE INN AT THE TAYLOR HOUSE

The Taylor House shortly after its construction in 1911. The only noticeable difference in the exterior today is the enclosed portion of the porch on the right side of the house, which contains the expanded dining room.

COURTESY OF CHIP SCHWAB

C. D. "Squire" Taylor was a prosperous farmer and entrepreneur. The builder of the Mast General Store, he later constructed the competing store now operated as the Mast Store Annex. The Taylors farmed most of the "upper" valley region, where they built and operated a mill that served local farmers. Squire Taylor's financial support helped build many of the roads in the valley, providing better access to the outside world.

Squire also played a significant role in the rebirth of the Episcopal mission at the turn of the century. By the late 1800s, he owned much of the original mission property, which had been sold decades earlier. Squire Taylor gave three acres of the original property back to the church, and the mission began another century of service in "the Valle."

The Inn at the Taylor House

Inn at the Taylor House

architectural beauty to the hidden valley. Though railroads brought wealth and access to building materials to mountain towns such as Asheville, Valle Crucis builders remained handicapped by their isolation. But you'd never know it looking at the romantic Inn at the Taylor House.

Like other local families, the Taylors opened their home as a summer inn. A flier described the opportunity this way: "If you are tired of busy days, a crowded city and bustling traffic, you can have a real vacation—one that is different—away from summer throngs!"

Today, those staying at the inn still appreciate Squire's design. As visitors did decades ago, guests enjoy breakfast in the airy dining room, where they are warmed by the morning sun. Toward midmorning, the broad porches, multiple dormers, and tall windows surrounding the house capture the light and make the best of both winter sun and summer breezes.

Under the elegant hand of current innkeeper Chip Schwab, the inn was honored with inclusion in *The Innkeepers' Register*, a fitting honor for a special place. The wide wraparound porch is filled with wicker chairs, and the rooms have views of the surrounding lush gardens and the valley's broad meadows. Inside, the tastefully restored farmhouse is filled with elegant furniture, rugs, and art. As soon as you step on the porch, you start looking for a place to take a nap.

Chip's breakfasts are legendary. A former cooking-school instructor, she is likely to start breakfast in the airy dining room with sour-cream crepes covered with strawberries, blueberries, or other local fruit in season, to be followed by a dish made from locally raised eggs.

Whether you pick out your favorite chair outside on the porch or in a private corner in the comfortable house, there is no better place to appreciate the beauty and history of Valle Crucis and to watch your worries disappear.

Just up the mountain from the Inn at the Taylor House sits a hallowed, mysterious site. To a person who happens to be driving by, the sign reading "Valle Crucis Conference Center at the Historic Mission School" says little. Behind the simple wooden sign, a strange jumble of buildings sits quietly on the hillside overlooking the meadows where the first missionaries arrived in the 1840s. The largest building, its giant front porch lined with rocking chairs, appears to be either a monastery, a hotel, or an ancient dormitory. Each is partially true.

CATALPA SHADOWS

The Valle Crucis Conference Center

VALLE CRUCIS EPISCOPAL MISSION

When Bishop Levi Ives traveled from Asheville to Valle Crucis in August 1843, he found few people. And those few people were, in his estimation, "poor, ignorant, but simple, honest, and kindly, though very quiet and un-demonstrative in manner."

Ives set out to establish what would become an important and long-lasting mission site for the Episcopal Church. He purchased almost everything he could see in the small valley and began building a sawmill, a kitchen, a dining room, a schoolroom, a dormitory, a chapel, and a bishop's house. In 1845, a school for thirty boys opened. Under the leadership of a director and a handful of candidates for the ministry, the mission was expected to cover a broad geographical region. Its purpose was to bring the backward pioneers to God.

The school was not an immediate success. Several boys were placed in the care of the missionaries with the hope of correcting recurring discipline problems, but unruly behavior resulted in the expulsion of some students and the withdrawal of others.

Yet the mission continued. William West Skiles, hired to supervise a growing farm operation, became the shining star of the Valle Crucis Episcopal Mission. Skiles prepared for the ministry, taught school, and was ordained a deacon by Bishop Ives in 1847. As a divinity student, Skiles was responsible for using his skills to minister to the special needs of the uneducated local population.

By 1847, the school for boys was disbanded, though the divinity school and the mission remained. The divinity students continued to do good works, hold services, and expand the mission into surrounding areas. That same year, Bishop Ives planned the Society of the Holy Cross, a monastic institution to be connected to the divinity school. Members of the society were to take vows of chastity, poverty, and obedience. Many of the divinity students, including William Skiles, joined the society, which was the first Anglican monastic order created since the Reformation in the mid-sixteenth century, when the Church of England broke from the Roman Catholic Church.

But dark clouds were gathering over the Diocese of North Carolina. The Episcopal Church grew concerned that the Society of the Holy Cross was straying from the teachings of the church and that Bishop Ives was teaching Roman Catholic practices such as private confes-

Valle Cruces Industrial School, Valle Cruces, N. C.

Valle Crucis Industrial School, early 1900s. On the left is Bishop Ives's cabin, far from its present site near the Main Building. The Main Building and Auxiliary Hall are at center. On the far right is the Mission House, the first building constructed when the mission was revived in 1895. The long, narrow buildings in the foreground are chicken houses.

VALLE CRUCIS CONFERENCE CENTER

sion. After two years of letters and meetings between Ives and church authorities, the last divinity student left and Bishop Ives disbanded the order. In ill health, he soon asked for a leave of absence from the church and sailed to Europe. Within two months, he resigned as bishop of North Carolina and declared his intent to join the Roman Catholic Church. He died the next year.

Bishop Ives owned much of the mission land and was heavily in debt. Shortly before his res-

ignation, his representatives had sold the property to a local farmer. While the buildings fell into ruin over the next decade, the Reverend Skiles remained in a small cabin at the mission and continued to preach, teach, and act as guardian to his flock. He held services at over a dozen locations as far away as Wilkesboro and Lenoir. Known far and wide for his kindness and generosity, he acted as doctor, counselor, and friend to those who could neither read nor write.

After Skiles's death, the mission and the

The Valle Crucis Conference Center

Episcopal churches in Valle Crucis hosted only visiting ministers who passed through every few years. However, St. John's Episcopal Church continued to function, and visiting preachers found a growing congregation there.

In 1883, Joseph Blount Cheshire became the new bishop of North Carolina. He vowed to reclaim and restore the hallowed mission. By that time, most of the original mission property was owned by the Taylor family, builders of the present-day Inn at the Taylor House, which sits down the road from the mission. All the original buildings except Bishop Ives's cabin, which still stands in front of the Church of the Holy Cross, were in ruins. Bishop Cheshire sought out the Reverend Milnor Jones, another missionary devoted to serving the mountain poor. Jones came to Valle Crucis, then headed north in search of donations to rebuild the mission.

Within a year, new construction began. The

IVES HOUSE TEA ROOM
Valle Crucis Home Crafts League
VALLE CRUCIS, N.C.

Taylor family donated three acres of the original mission property. The Reverend Jones first built the Mission House, which stands today behind the red-colored Apple Barn. The Mission House was home to a new teacher, a classroom, and a dormitory.

Other workers followed. The mission established a boarding school for girls. A new chapel—now the Day Care Center—doubled as a classroom. By the turn of the century, the mission had bought over five hundred acres of its original property back from the Taylors, including the

The Main Building (left) and Auxiliary Hall (right) in the early 1900s

VALLE CRUCIS CONFERENCE CENTER

Exterior of the Chapel of the Holy Cross, which sits near the Mission House and Apple Barn. Constructed in 1902 as a chapel and classroom for the revived mission, it is almost unrecognizable today as the Day Care Center.

VALLE CRUCIS CONFERENCE CENTER

Interior of the Chapel of the Holy Cross

VALLE CRUCIS CONFERENCE CENTER

broad meadows now grazed by cattle. By 1903, donations allowed the construction of Auxiliary Hall, now the Dining Hall.

A new, dedicated leader, Bishop Junius Horner, then took the reins. In response to Bishop Horner's plans to make the mission self-sufficient, workers planted orchards and built a sawmill, chicken houses, and a wagon factory. Under the direction of Mary Horner, the bishop's wife, the mission school became recognized as

The dining and assembly room in the Dining Hall, 1938. It appears much the same today.
VALLE CRUCIS CONFERENCE CENTER

During the tenure of Bishops Cheshire and Horner, the mission school developed an income-producing farm operation. One of the school's primary crops was apples, which the students helped harvest.
VALLE CRUCIS CONFERENCE CENTER

Students enjoying the fruits of their labor
VALLE CRUCIS CONFERENCE CENTER

Students of the Valle Crucis School performing at a school picnic

VALLE CRUCIS CONFERENCE CENTER

Basketball on the grounds below the Main Building sometime between 1919 and 1921. The chimney in the upper right is a remnant of Auxiliary Hall, which burned.

COURTESY OF BILL AND MARILYN WELCH

The school choir preparing for church. The building in the background, Auxiliary Hall, stood on the site of the current Dining Hall.

VALLE CRUCIS CONFERENCE CENTER

Schoolgirls in a simple dorm room
of the Main Building, 1938
VALLE CRUCIS CONFERENCE CENTER

Students in front of the dairy barn on the mission school's
farm, early 1900s. The building is known
today as the Apple Barn.
VALLE CRUCIS CONFERENCE CENTER

the best school in the area. By 1908, its rolls included about a hundred boarders and day students. Initially known as the Valle Crucis Industrial School to distinguish it from the local public school, it later was known simply as the Valle Crucis School. Students arrived from throughout the eastern United States. Thanks to the mission's success, students and charitable donations came in steadily.

The year 1908 also saw the construction of the mission's largest building, now known as the Main Building. The Main Building served as a self-contained dormitory with a chapel, a library, an office, and a laundry. It stands unchanged today, its magnificent, 110-foot-long front porch lined with rocking chairs.

During the next decade, Bishop Horner oversaw the construction of a dairy barn—now the Apple Barn—and a hydroelectric plant far up Crab Orchard Creek. This plant lit the mission buildings and much of the surrounding valley. Heat, however, was still provided by fires and giant boilers. As was often the case when open fires were the sole source of heat, buildings burned, including the sawmill and the wagon factory. When Auxiliary Hall burned in 1919, a teacher and a young student tragically died. The structure was later rebuilt.

By 1925, Valle Crucis had outgrown the small chapel than now serves as the Day Care Center. In order to accommodate the growing congregation and to replace the old chapel, constructed in 1895, the diocese built the Church of the Holy Cross.

The Great Depression hit the mission as it did the rest of the country. By 1934, the national church withdrew its much-needed financial support. The school struggled until 1942, when it closed. The orchards and farm remained in operation, but the mission itself was forced to adapt in order to survive. After World War II, it began operating again as a training ground for seminary students, a role it filled for the next two decades.

WAITING FOR VISITORS

The Valle Crucis Conference Center

Holy Cross cemetery

Visitors here are on the grounds of a century-and-a-half-old Episcopal mission, one of the country's best-preserved. Presiding over the site is the beautiful, stone Church of the Holy Cross. The mission was once surrounded by apple orchards and teemed with missionaries and students. Its struggles and accomplishments are woven throughout the history of the last century and a half of "the Valle."

IN THE VALLEY OF THE CROSS

Church of the Holy Cross

Its history is also woven into that of my own family. During the early 1900s, my grandmother attended school here. The presiding bishop's wife, Mary Horner, was her teacher and principal. My grandmother fondly remembered playing basketball in a skirt with other schoolgirls on the small, level area below the great front porch. Educated in a living nature museum, the girls often took field trips to the surrounding mountains. In addition to doing their schoolwork, they learned to cook, weave, and worship. My father still has my grandmother's fifth-grade report card from the Valle Crucis Industrial School, where she received grades for cooking, laundry work, housework, sewing, grammar, reading, arithmetic, history, and geography. The report card, dated 1914, was signed by Mary E. Horner, principal.

It was in 1925 that the Episcopal diocese built the Church of the Holy Cross. My grandparents were the first couple married here. The church is topped by a three-thousand-pound Celtic cross dedicated to Bishop Joseph Blount Cheshire. Inside the church, which looks like it came straight out of an English village, visitors can still see the remarkable chair made for Bishop Ives in the mid-1800s from gnarled rhododendron branches. The church floor is constructed of two-by-four-inch blocks of wood. In the small foyer inside the front door, you can see a stained-glass window depicting a St. Andrew's cross as formed by the creeks of the valley.

PRAYER IN STONE

Church of the Holy Cross

Church of the Holy Cross

BISHOP'S CHAIRS

Church of the Holy Cross

FLOWERS FOR THE SEASON

Church of the Holy Cross

The Cottage, Valle Crucis Conference Center

A small outdoor chapel sits in the woods on the hillside below the church. In the late 1940s, the church's youth group solicited stones from churches around the world for the construction of the altar in the outdoor chapel. My father, in the youth group at the time, wrote letters in pursuit of those stones. On warm summer days, services were held outside in the shady chapel.

By the late 1960s, the diocese converted the mission school into a conference center. In the 1970s, it found new life as the site of the Summer Youth Program, which brought youths from throughout the country to serve the mission and the people of the region. This program was responsible for the renovation of many of the mission's buildings. Several of the young adults who attended the Summer Youth Program remained in Valle Crucis or returned later to live here.

Groups of all kinds are still drawn to the sacred site. In 1992, the mission school and the Church of the Holy Cross celebrated the mission's 150th anniversary. The next year, in recognition of a century and a half of struggle and good works, the mission school was placed on the National Register of Historic Places.

Each summer until her death, my grandmother and I eagerly awaited the return of the musicians of the North American Bagpiping School, who spent a week each year at the mission school filling the valley with music. Each Sunday, after I attend the church where my grandparents were married, I choose a rocking chair on the long front porch of the Main Building, and sit. After a while, I can almost hear the sounds of my grandmother and her schoolmates playing below.

The Shull's family cemetery (1979)

VALLE CRUCIS

December on the Watauga River

Near the Watauga River (1977)

The Hodges farm (1983)

READY FOR CURING

Staked tobacco, Highway 194

VALLE CRUCIS

In many an old barn

Baird's Creek area

The Watauga River

Walker Valley

VALLE CRUCIS

The lower River Road

If you'd like to see Valle Crucis at its most vibrant, try visiting during the Valle Country Fair.

Before dawn on the second Saturday of October, something remarkable happens. Lights go on in a large red barn just below the Valle Crucis Conference Center. A few people start milling around the grassy area surrounding the barn.

APPLE BUTTER TIME

Apple butter at the Valle Country Fair

As the sun rises, the upstanding members of the Church of the Holy Cross start building fires. On these fires are placed giant, aged cast-iron pots. From these pots, the smells of apple butter and Brunswick stew slowly coax the valley to life.

Soon thereafter, the first truckload of frost-chilled apples arrives. You can watch them being crushed into sparkling, sweet apple cider in the old hand-turned wooden press that has blistered my own hands. After weeks of preparation, Valle Crucis residents are ready for an onslaught of visitors unmatched throughout the year. If you stand around long enough, you might get a chance to pitch in.

By the time the morning sun begins to warm the frost, you can see some of the best craftsmen in the country displaying their art. You can find the finest of quilts, furniture, dried flowers, toys, dolls, paintings, photography, pottery, weavings, jewelry, and other wares. What began as a small church fair has grown to a festival known throughout the Southeast for its excellence.

To avoid the crowds, arrive early. Both the church and the valley have been overwhelmed by interest in this small mountain fair. There is a waiting list among artisans hoping to set up booths in the small field surrounding the Apple Barn—and with good cause. In recent years, attendance at the fair has grown to 15,000 people. More than 150 carefully selected artisans are chosen by a church committee for their special talents and are given the chance to participate in the fair.

Some people come for the food, some for the music, and some for the square dancing. In the spirit of a true country fair, local residents load tables with homemade jams, jellies, breads, and cakes. Apple cider is sold or drunk on the spot by the gallon. People gather around the big pots of apple butter sniffing and reminiscing about breakfasts past, then load up their cars with jars of the stuff.

After you have emptied your wallet and filled your stomach, you can sit and listen to some of the area's best music. Whether you like bluegrass, ballads, traditional dulcimer music, or barbershop quartets, you will find yourself smiling and tapping your toe. And if you stick around

Valle Country Fair

until dark, you can brush up on your square dancing. If you don't know how, there is no better place to learn. On the worn wooden floors of the Apple Barn, you can learn enough steps to have a good time.

When the crowds have gone home, the Valle Country Fair begins to serve its true purpose. Proceeds from the first fair helped build a much-needed church meeting facility, Skiles Hall. On an honor system, all artisans now contribute a portion of their earnings to the church, which distributes the proceeds to such organizations as Habitat for Humanity, the Watauga County Hunger Coalition, Avery County Project Literacy, the Watauga County Humane Society, and the Boy Scouts. From its beginning, the fair has existed to serve the needs of the less fortunate and to celebrate and preserve those things that make Valle Crucis a unique place.

AN UNCOMMON CLARITY

Dutch Creek Valley

Dutch Creek Valley

Indeed, the local pride and community concern in evidence at the Valle Country Fair permeate life in Valle Crucis. Author Philip Larkin once said that "the impulse to preserve lies at the bottom of all art." In my case, that turns out to be true. I have always been drawn by the beauty of Valle Crucis, by its sacred past. I am determined to do my part to prevent its disappearance.

The rest of the world has now found Valle Crucis, and it is in danger of being destroyed by its beauty. On almost every weekend of the year, it swarms with visitors. Traffic clogs the narrow roads. Even more ominous are the circling real-estate developers, the skyrocketing property values, the houses elbowing for hillside spots with the best view. The lights of ridge-top mansions pierce the once-dark night.

FINE MORNING COMING

Shull's Farm (1983)

As this book reaches publication, a spirited debate is taking place over whether to widen old bridges and redesign the elegant, historic road that sneaks through the woods from Valle Crucis past the mission school to Banner Elk. To those who live in or love "the Valle," the issue is emotional. The road, a survivor of decades of harsh winters, may be destroyed to accommodate

TOUCH-ME-NOTS

Dutch Creek Road

Toward Beech Mountain

more visitors—most of whom would have marveled at the craftsmanship of the early road builders. The road is as much a part of the character of the valley as are the mountains, the streams, the mission school, the inns, the churches, and the Mast General Store. My own view is that destroying the historic road to accommodate more cars would be as great a sin as replacing the Mast General Store with a mall to shove in more shoppers.

In the broad "lower" valley, the once-clear water of the Watauga faces danger from upstream development. With little government control, developers are tripping over themselves to subdivide farms and build homes closer and closer together in anticipation of more and more visitors. Wastewater from upstream development has polluted the river. Eventually, the valley's magnificent mountains, its quiet meadows, its isolation—everything that has drawn visitors here for a century—might disappear under the crush of progress. And after Valle Crucis's beauty has disappeared, visitors will no longer have a reason to come here.

The debate between preservation and development is not a new one. However, we all know what happens when unfettered development ravages a community. We also know how planning can save a small area from the wounds of condos, neon signs, and "shoppes."

Fortunately, some local residents are showing the foresight to protect "the Valle." The Valle Crucis Historic District, created in 1990, has gained some control over building, but only in a limited geographical area. Historic districts are creations of law. They exist to preserve important historic structures and the special character of historic areas. They are a form of zoning intended to prevent important structures from being demolished and to prevent factories and modern office buildings from being constructed beside places like the Mast General Store.

When an area is designated a historic district, a historic commission is elected and is responsible for drafting an ordinance and enforcing that ordinance. The Valle Crucis ordinance allows the commission to enforce guidelines concerning such things as signs and the appearance, size, and location of buildings. For instance, new buildings in the historic district should be of the same general style as the existing buildings. The ordinance does not stop development. It can only attempt to control the way it looks.

The boundary of the Valle Crucis Historic District encompasses roughly the area between the Mast Farm Inn and the Mast General Store in the "lower" valley and the area surrounding the mission school in the "upper" valley. In the rest of the valley, there is no protection.

AUTUMN BELOW GRANDFATHER

Shull's Mill *area*

Toward Grandfather Mountain

Preacher Billings Road

In our ever-expanding world, few places make us feel safe and at home. In our cities and neighborhoods, we try to create something that feels like the safe, friendly places where we grew up. We try to create places like Valle Crucis.

My hope is that, having seen this book, people will bring with them a love and respect for "the Valle" and a determination to preserve it. Whether through legal controls or existing or new nonprofit groups, it can be done. It has been done elsewhere. Concerned residents have successfully preserved similar rural tourist areas from rampant development. Nantucket Island, Massachusetts, like Valle Crucis, is small, old, remote, beautiful, and swarming with tourists. However, thanks to a combination of legal controls and nonprofit conservation groups, the fragile landscape and historic structures of Nantucket Island are protected from those who would exploit them—all without trampling personal rights. Like cherished structures, cherished land, too, can be protected.

But preservation requires vigorous support. Please do your part to protect this beautiful place. As you watch the fog rise in the valley on a cool summer morning, shuffle through its bright autumn leaves, or sit on the porch during a silent, moonlit snowfall, vow to make sure this place remains for your children.

Grandfather Mountain